big brands

AMAZON

Adam Sutherland

WAYLAND

contents

the everything store

button will not display if:

- It is not available in your country of residence or location.
- Your device is not yet registered.

Menu: Tap to display a list of options. The menus are contextual, which means they change to offer appropriate options depending on what you're currently doing with the device. For example, on the Home screen of a Kindle with Special Offers, menu options may include Shop in Kindle Store, View Special Offers, Kindle FreeTime, Vocabulary Builder, Experimental Browser, Settings, List or Cover View, Create New Collection, and Sync and Check for Items. Note that you can view content on the Home screen using the default cover view or by list view.

When you're reading a book, menu

Loc 91   12%

The Kindle, with its huge library of digital content, has captured a new and rapidly growing market for Amazon.

What can you not buy on Amazon? From a sailor suit for your cat (£5.50) to a top-of-the range Samsung 4K television (£2,098), Amazon stocks virtually anything and everything you can think of, and will deliver it to your door in just a few hours.

In 2012, its 17th year of business, the company passed $61bn (£38.5bn) in annual sales, employed over 100,000 people (compared to Google's 50,000 and Facebook's 7,000), and is on course to be the fastest retailer to reach $100bn (£63bn) in sales.

But, like many businesses, the road to Amazon's current success has been full of twists and turns. The company – founded by Jeff Bezos (pronounced 'Bay-zose') – started as a simple online bookseller that rode the first wave of dotcom enthusiasm in the late 1990s to expand into selling music, films, electronics and toys.

Narrowly avoiding disaster following the dotcom bust of 2000 and 2001, it modernised its distribution network, and diversified again into software, jewellery, clothes, sporting goods and more. Then, having established itself as the Internet's top retailer, it extended its influence into technology with Amazon

> If you want to get to the truth about what makes us different, it's this: we are genuinely customer-centric, we are genuinely long-term oriented and we genuinely like to invent. Most companies are not those things. They are focused on the competitor, rather than the customer… And they prefer to be close-followers rather than inventors, because it's safer.

Jeff Bezos

Web Services' cloud computing, and digital devices like the Kindle, Kindle Fire tablet and now the Fire Phone.

Amazon is innovative, and has changed the way the world views eCommerce. It's not the financial powerhouse of Google, or even Facebook, however. By striving to put the customer first, and offering everyday low prices, company profit margins are small, and the company actually made a loss as recently as 2012. But there is no doubt that Amazon has made, and will continue to make, a significant impact on the way we shop.

Business Matters
eCommerce

The Internet enables us to shop from our computers, and even from our mobiles. Businesses can trade around the world without the need to open physical stores, leading to lower costs. Computer programs allow these businesses to learn lots of information about their customers, and their buying habits.

Since 2010, Amazon has invested over £9bn to build 50 new warehouses, like this one outside Berlin, Germany.

the birth of the business

Jeff Bezos
Founder of Amazon

A gifted maths and science student in high school, Bezos graduated from the University of Princeton in 1986 with a degree in electrical engineering and computer science. He worked in investment banking on New York's Wall Street before launching Amazon. His drive, ideas and refusal to give anything less than his best has seen him named *Time* magazine's Person of the Year (1999), and Businessperson of the Year by *Fortune* (2012), as well as one of the richest people on the planet!

A mazon founder Jeff Bezos got a taste for the possibilities of the Internet while working for investment bankers D.E. Shaw & Co in New York. David Shaw and Bezos often discussed the idea of an 'everything store' – an Internet company that served as a middleman between customers and manufacturers and sold just about any type of product, all over the world.

Bezos started to research the business, and discovered that Internet activity was growing at a massive 230,000% year on year! The young entrepreneur became convinced that he needed to launch a new business to take advantage of this opportunity.

Making a list of 20 possible product categories, he quickly decided on books for two main reasons: 1) there were just two main book distributors in the US, so a new retailer would only have to approach two companies, instead of thousands of individual publishers; 2) at the time there were 3 million books in print worldwide – far more than any bricks and mortar bookstore could stock.

Amazon had its USP – an unlimited selection of titles. 'With that huge diversity of [titles] you could build a store online that simply could not exist in any other way,' Bezos remembers. 'You could build a true superstore with exhaustive selection, and customers value selection.'

Bezos quickly put his plans into action, leaving D.E. Shaw & Co to pursue his dreams. But where would he have his HQ? Because US law stated that businesses did not have to collect sales tax in states they did not have physical operations (for example, offices or warehouses), Bezos chose Seattle, in the Pacific Northwest, rather than heavily populated states such as California or New York.

In 1994 the company name Cadabra Inc was registered, along with other domain names including Browse.com, Bookmall.com and Relentless.com (try Relentless.com and see where it takes you today!).

Business Matters
The Unique Selling Proposition (USP)

A USP is some unique quality about a company's product or service that will attract customers to use or buy it rather than a competitor's. As a 'virtual book store', Amazon's USP was its huge range of titles that couldn't be found in any one physical store.

Investing
in the future

Shel Kaphan
Amazon's first employee

A maths graduate from the University of California, computer programmer Kaphan met Jeff Bezos when the future Amazon CEO was still working at D.E. Shaw & Co. When Amazon was formed, Kaphan joined the new company as Chief Technology Officer (CTO), building Amazon's first website from scratch, and staying with the company until 1999.

The Amazon homepage – more than just a bookstore.

B ezos knew he needed a more memorable company name and, searching through the dictionary, came across the word 'Amazon': the world's largest river. What better name for the world's largest bookstore? On 1 November 1994, Bezos registered the URL – Amazon.com was born!

In Amazon's earliest days, Bezos funded the company with his own savings, putting in nearly $100,000 (£64,000) in the first two years. His parents invested a further $100,000 – even though Bezos told them there was a 70 per cent chance they could lose it all!

The Amazon website launched on 16 July 1995 – proudly proclaiming 'One million titles, consistently low prices'. It contained a virtual shopping basket, a simple search engine, and a secure credit card payment system. But that's where the similarities with today's site end. In the early days, when someone bought a book, a bell would ring on employees' computers and everyone gathered round to see if they knew the buyer!

Amazon held no stock itself, so it would order the book from a distributor, wait for delivery, and then ship it to the customer. Most books took a week to reach Amazon, far longer for harder-to-find items, so the company was always struggling to stay on top of orders. The first week after launch, Amazon took $12,000 (£7,700) in orders, and shipped just $846 (£540) of books.

Business Matters
Company logo

Company logos are a graphic representation of a company's name, designed to promote instant recognition. When Amazon first launched, its logo was a giant A on a blue background with a graphic of a river snaking through it. Today's more sophisticated design combines the company's full name with an arrow running from A to Z. The curved arrow is also designed to look like a smile.

Press coverage boosted brand awareness and therefore sales. By the start of 1996, revenues were growing 30–40 per cent a month, but profit margins were slim. Amazon paid distributors a standard 50 per cent of the retail price, but offered up to a 40 per cent discount on bestsellers. Huge volumes of sales were needed for Amazon to truly fulfil its potential. But that meant putting even more pressure on a young company that was struggling to keep on top of ever-increasing demand.

The vast Amazon river, inspiration for Jeff Bezos' 'everything store'.

Amazon goes public

Like many dotcoms, Amazon's rapid growth didn't mean immediate profits. In 1996 the company generated $15.7m (£10m) in sales, but made a loss of $5.8m (£3.7m).

More investment was urgently needed. Silicon Valley venture capital firm Kleiner Perkins invested $8m (£5.1m) for a 13 per cent share of the company, adding essential funds for investment in more staff, distribution centres, and computing power.

Bezos' new motto was Get Big Fast. The bigger Amazon grew, he reasoned, the lower prices it could negotiate with book wholesalers, and the more distribution capacity it could invest in to get books delivered faster and cheaper. The Amazon founder was in a race to be one of the biggest and best brands in the new digital marketplace, because he believed it would also protect him from increased competition. 'When you are small,' he once explained, 'someone else [who] is bigger can always come along and take away what you have.'

The drive to be bigger led to Amazon's IPO (Initial Public Offering, where shares in a private company are sold on the Stock Exchange) in May 1997. The company raised $54m (£34.5m) – turning Bezos, his parents and other early investors into multimillionaires overnight. More importantly, though, it provided more funds to invest in the company's continued growth, and worldwide publicity that boosted annual revenues by a massive 900 per cent year on year.

When companies grow so fast, recruitment can be a problem – not just hiring enough staff to cope with the growth, but hiring the right people. To this day, recruitment at Amazon follows a pattern that Bezos learned while working for D.E. Shaw in New York. After an interview, everyone involved in the hiring process expresses one of four opinions: strong no hire; inclined not to hire; inclined to hire; or strong hire. Just one negative view can fail a candidate. 'Every time we hire someone', Bezos explained to colleagues, 'he or she should raise the bar for the next hire, so that the overall talent pool is always improving.'

Rise in Value of Internet IPO Shares

Amazon.com
$1,000 in 1997 - **$239,045** today

ebay
$1,000 in 1998 - **$68,638** today

YAHOO!
$1,000 in 1996 - **$61,052** today

Google
$1,000 in 2004 - **$12,072** today

Linkedin
$1,000 in 2011 - **$4,972** today

facebook
$1,000 in 2012 - **$1,269** today

Business Matters
Initial Public Offering (IPO)

An IPO, or stock market launch, allows shares of stock in a company to be sold to investors, including the general public. The process transforms a private company into a public company and is mainly used by companies to raise funds to enable them to expand and grow the business.

dotcom boom and bust

Business Matters
Profit and Loss

A company's financial report, also known as a profit and loss statement, shows how the revenue (money received from the sale of products and services before expenses are taken out) is transformed into the net income (the result after all revenues and expenses have been accounted for). It shows the revenues for a specific period, and the cost and expenses charged against those revenues. The purpose of the report is to show company managers and investors whether the company made or lost money during a specific period.

Books were never going to be Amazon's sole focus. A key part of the company's early strategy was maximising the Internet's ability to provide a superior selection of products compared with traditional retail stores.

Management teams were charged with researching products with high SKUs (the number of potentially stockable items) that were under-represented in physical stores, and could be sent easily through the post. Early additions were CDs, DVDs, toys and electronics.

Adding more product categories meant more warehouses were needed to house all the new stock. Between 1998 and early 2000, Amazon raised an incredible $2.2bn (£1.4bn) in further investment, opening five new distribution centres, recruiting new staff (the company grew from 1,500 employees in 1998 to 7,600 at the start of 2000), financing deals with AOL, Yahoo and other sites to be their exclusive online bookseller, and purchasing a number of existing online businesses – including Pets.com, Drugstore.com

Tom Szkutak
Amazon Chief Financial Officer (CFO)

Szkutak studied finance at Boston University before joining General Electric Co. He ran international finance operations for the company before joining Amazon in 2002. Szkutak, who retires in summer 2015, oversees all of Amazon's financial activities – keeping an eye on budgets, making sure the company is paying the correct tax, and informing investors about company financial performance.

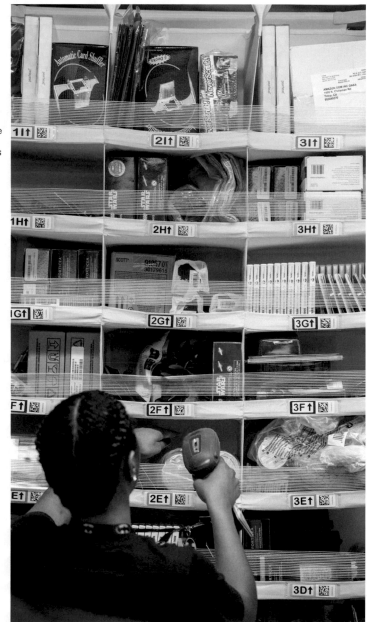

An Amazon employee scans items in preparation for 'Cyber Monday' – one of the busiest shopping days of the year.

and Home-grocer.com – in efforts to achieve Bezos' ambition to be 'the everything store'.

This ambition came at a cost. Although sales were up 95 per cent year on year in 1999, Amazon was left with $39m (£24.9m) in unsold toys after Christmas that year, and many of Bezos' acquisitions failed to thrive within Amazon. Most eventually closed, costing the company hundreds of millions of dollars. Amazon was on track to lose a massive $1bn (£638m) in 2000!

On top of this came the dotcom crash of 2000, when stock markets around the world radically reappraised the value of Internet companies with millions of dollars in turnover, but no profits. Investors stopped lending against the promise of future earnings, and many companies went bust.

Fortunately for Amazon, a healthy bank balance meant there wasn't an urgent need for more funding, so the company cut back further expansion plans, concentrating instead on reducing costs, improving its distribution network, and aiming to be profitable as soon as possible.

beating the... competition

Establishing a successful company rarely happens without competition. In Amazon's case, it took on bookselling giant Barnes and Noble in the US, and won!

The long-established book chain had notched up $2bn (£1.27bn) in sales in 1996, compared to Amazon's tiny $16m (£10.2m), but was nevertheless wary of the newcomer's growing appeal. The Barnes and Noble owners met with Bezos and his team to sound out a deal to buy Amazon. The offer was never made, however, and Barnes and Noble eventually decided to launch a rival website.

The corporate giants were disastrously slow to market, allowing Amazon the time not only to expand their customer base but also to add important innovations to the site.

Bezos believed that if Amazon had more user-generated book reviews, it would give them a huge advantage. Publishers complained when they saw bad reviews of their books, but Bezos stood firm. 'We don't make money when we sell things,' he explained to one publisher. 'We make money when we help customers make purchase decisions.'

Another idea that helped Amazon stand out was the idea of 1-Click ordering. Bezos told programmers he wanted to make it as easy as possible for customers to buy things on the site, so they devised a system that preloaded a customer's credit card details and a preferred shipping address, and then offered them the chance to make a purchase with a single press of a button. Not only had Amazon simplified a buying process that could lead to millions more dollars in orders, but by filing a patent on the technology, it also prevented other companies copying the process!

Building the Brand
First mover advantage

Companies who enter a particular market – in Amazon's case, online bookselling – before any competitors can often gain important advantages. They have the opportunity to develop customer loyalty and brand recognition, get access to investment funding, and develop new technologies ahead of their rivals.

Business Matters
Core Values

The fundamental beliefs which guide a business are called its core values. They help a business set its goals and decide on actions. Amazon's core values were defined by Bezos in 1998 and are:
* Customer obsession
* Frugality
* Bias for action
* Ownership
* High bar for talent
* Innovation

Barnes & Noble reacted too slowly to the growth of online retailing, allowing Amazon to thrive with little competition.

the competitive edge

As early as 1997, Amazon was looking at the success of auction site eBay and trying to incorporate third-party sellers into Amazon, with commission from every sale helping to boost company profits.

Toys 'R' Us have used Amazon's distribution network to reach their own customers.

> "There are two kinds of retailers: there are those folks who work to figure how to charge more, and there are companies that work to figure how to charge less, and we are going to be the second, full-stop.

Jeff Bezos, July 2008

In 2000, Bezos began telling colleagues that by the time Amazon reached $200bn (£127bn) in sales, he expected revenue to be split equally between what Amazon sold itself, and commission from other sellers using the site.

The same year, Amazon announced a deal with Toys 'R' Us to be their exclusive online partner. The toy retailer would use its experience to choose the right toys for each season, and negotiate low prices with manufacturers. Amazon would attract the maximum number of online customers, and ship products on time. Similar deals followed with AOL's shopping channel, electronics retailer Century City, and even book chain Borders.

All these partnerships were short-lived, however, as Bezos' obsession with offering customers the lowest possible prices and the widest choice created tension with other retailers. Amazon Marketplace, which launched in November 2000, raised protests from American publishers' and authors' organisations, because the sales of used books affected the purchase of new ones, and reduced author royalties. Even Amazon staff objected as Marketplace effectively meant they could lose sales to competition from within their own website!

Nevertheless, Bezos' plan worked. In 2002, sales from third-party sellers made up 33% of company revenues, marketing costs were reduced, international revenues were up, and Amazon finally posted its first profitable quarter – $5m (£3.2m). In the first quarter of 2003, Amazon amassed $1bn (£636m) in sales for the first time during a non-holiday period. Third-party sellers – in everything from books to kettles to televisions – continue to boost Amazon's revenue to this day.

Even fellow bookseller Borders used Amazon's superior logistics, before their closure in 2011.

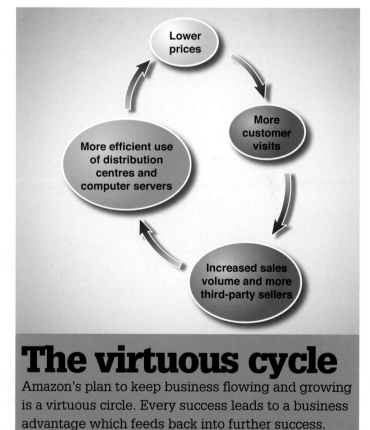

The virtuous cycle
Amazon's plan to keep business flowing and growing is a virtuous circle. Every success leads to a business advantage which feeds back into further success.

improving
the customer
experience

Amazon continued growing, expanding to 9,000 employees by the end of 2004. It also extended its worldwide reach – and increased sales – by launching a number of international sites, including www.amazon.cn (China), www.amazon.in (India), www.amazon.com.au (Australia) and www.amazon.com.br (Brazil).

Localised sites with more localised content is something that eCommerce is perfectly equipped to deliver, and Amazon used it as a way of expanding its customer base.

Another way of expanding the customer base, Bezos believed, was improving the customer experience. New features were added to the Amazon site, like the 'Search Inside the Book', which allows customers to search for words and phrases in a massive 100,000 books. Although publishers worried about online piracy, Bezos persevered and on its launch, technology magazine *Wired* ran a feature on Amazon, praising the company for its innovation.

What better way of improving the customer experience than offering free postage? When surveys showed that shipping costs were one of the biggest hurdles to ordering online, Amazon decided to offer free shipping for customers

The Star Wars DVD boxset is Amazon's best-selling pre-order item ever!

Jeff Wilke
Amazon troubleshooter

Computer whizz kid Wilke has a degree from Princeton and an MBS from the Massachusetts Institute of Technology (MIT). He joined Amazon in 1999, and his first job was correcting mistakes in the supply chain – making sure the correct orders went to the correct people, as quickly and efficiently as possible. Wilke stills works at Amazon where he is now Senior Vice President, Consumer Business.

Jeff Bezos introduces the Kindle Fire in 2011. The tablet can be used to access Amazon Prime Video – a video on-demand system to rival Netflix.

who were prepared to wait a few days for their purchases.

Eventually, Amazon Prime was introduced – a members' club with a £79 annual fee – that enabled free next-day shipping. Prime was a gamble that could have cost Amazon millions in profits: because the concept was untested, no one knew how many people would sign up, or if Prime would positively affect customer orders.

The high cost of next-day delivery lost the company money at first, but it slowly achieved the goal of making customers 'Amazon addicts', hooked on the almost instant gratification of receiving purchases so quickly. Prime gradually boosted customer spending to more than cover its costs, and has become a huge success – in fact, customers double their spending on the site on average when they become Prime members!

Business Matters
Diversification

Companies often decide to offer new products or services because it reduces the risk of its other products becoming too limited or boring. Amazon grew from an online bookstore to selling music, DVDs, toys, electronics, fashion and more. It became 'the everything store' that founder Jeff Bezos had always wanted.

Amazon's HQ, like the brand itself, is more functional and less space-age than Silicon Valley competitors such as Apple and Google.

Business Matters
Headhunting

Companies often find suitable candidates for vacant positions through a process of headhunting. Employees working in similar roles in other companies – often competitors – are approached, and offered the chance of a new position. This usually includes an increase in salary and a promotion to a more important position.

life at Amazon HQ

Bikes on Google's campus in Mountain View, California – a perk for employees.

The perks that dotcom employees often enjoy are legendary: free meals prepared by world-famous chefs, free transport to and from work and eye-poppingly futuristic offices. But Amazon is different. Aside from a bowl of dog biscuits by the front desk, for employees who bring their pets to the office, Amazon expects its employees to pay for snacks, and even office parking. The money the company saves, according to Bezos, is passed on to the customer in savings.

Occupying a dozen buildings south of Seattle's Lake Union, Amazon is also one of the few high-profile dotcom companies not based in California's Silicon Valley. Nevertheless, it still attracts some of the country's finest young thinkers, who often have to pass a baffling interview process. Bezos has been known to ask prospective candidates questions such as, 'How many [petrol] stations are in the United States?' He's not looking for the right answer, rather he wants candidates to show creativity by coming up with clever ways to work out a possible solution.

Once hired, even the most technically brilliant Amazon employees are not allowed use PowerPoint presentations to explain new products in team meetings. Instead, all staff write proposals, laying out their points in essay form, because Bezos believes it develops critical thinking. The goal is to present a new initiative – from a new product line on the website to a new Smartphone – in a clear, simple way that a customer might read if they were hearing about it for the first time.

Bezos makes his email address – jeff@amazon.com – available to all customers. He reads all the emails and forwards them to relevant executives with one addition – a question mark. Managers are expected to solve the problem and report back to Bezos within a few hours. If one customer has gone to the trouble of emailing him, Bezos believes, it's likely that hundreds if not thousands of others are experiencing the same problem. 'Every anecdote from a customer matters,' he says. 'We treat them as precious sources of information.'

> **There is so much stuff that has yet to be invented. There's so much new that's going to happen. People don't have any idea yet how impactful the Internet is going to be and that this is still Day 1 in such a big way.**
>
> **Jeff Bezos: Plaque on the wall in Amazon's Seattle HQ**

never standing still

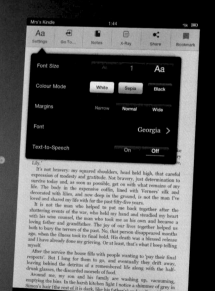

The Kindle Fire HD has helped Amazon take a slice of the lucrative tablet market.

Between 2003 and 2005, Amazon lost many of its most talented engineers to a fast-growing Google, who had opened offices just 20 minutes from Amazon's HQ. The success of the Google search engine also put a barrier between Amazon and its customers. Because web users started their searches through Google, rather than directly on Amazon, it meant that the site had to pay Google to advertise certain popular search terms like 'flat-screen TV' or 'Apple iPad'.

Bezos became convinced that he needed to transform Amazon from a simple online retailer to a technology company. 'There's only one way out of this predicament', he told employees at the time, 'and that is to invent our way out.' Here are Amazon's main inventions since then:

Amazon Web Services (AWS)

Amazon's original 'cloud computing' service sells storage, databases and computing power to a range of businesses – large and small. Pinterest and Instagram rent space on Amazon's computers, and Netflix uses AWS to stream films to its customers. Even more important, the CIA and NASA also use AWS's computing power to run their businesses. It's estimated that AWS generates around $2bn (£1.3bn) in annual revenues.

> " To me Amazon is a story of a brilliant founder who personally drove the vision. People forget that most people believed Amazon was doomed because it would not scale at a cost structure that would work… But Jeff was very smart. He's a classic technical founder of a business, who understands every detail and cares about it more than anyone. "
>
> **Eric Schmidt, former chairman of Google**

The Kindle (see also p24)

The original Kindle e-book reader was released in November 2007 and sold out in just five and a half hours. Kindles allow customers to buy books, newspapers and magazines from Amazon and download them through a form of wifi called Whispernet. In 2013, sales of the device reached 20 million, bringing in $3.9bn (£2.5bn) in revenue, with an additional $300-500m (£190-320m) in e-book sales per year.

The Kindle Fire

Amazon's version of a tablet computer combines an e-book reader with a colour screen to allow film viewing, with the functionality of a tablet for gaming and web surfing. The Kindle Fire launched in November 2011 in the US, and quickly became the second best-selling tablet on the market after Apple's iPad. Although sales figures have never been released, experts estimate around 10-11m Kindle Fires are sold every year – this compared to roughly 50m iPads sold annually.

The Fire Phone

This 3D-enabled phone is Amazon's entry into the lucrative smartphone market. Released in July 2014, experts believe it has not been as commercially successful as the Kindle or Kindle Fire. Prices started at $200 (£130) for a 32Gb version – similar price to an iPhone 5s or Samsung GS5 and sales are believed to be under 40,000 devices.

Business Matters
Fulfilment

eCommerce businesses have to master the process of fulfilment – registering customer orders, taking secure payment and delivering goods promptly. In the run-up to Christmas 2013, Amazon sold an amazing 426 items per second! A fast and efficient fulfilment system was vital to ensure orders were delivered in time.

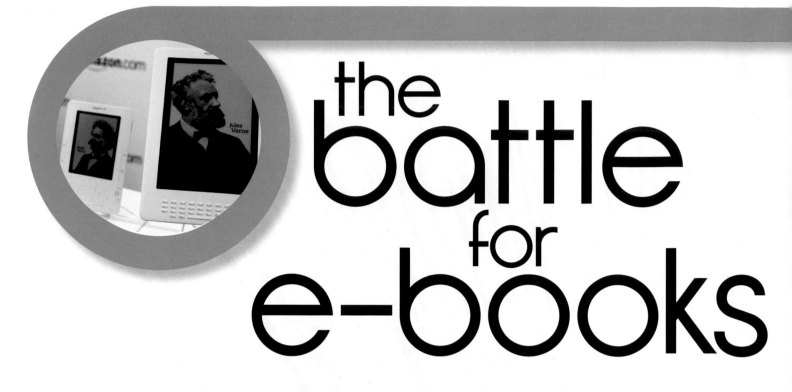

the battle for e-books

Following the launch of iTunes and the iPod, Apple leapfrogged Amazon and Walmart to become the top music retailer in the US. With 74 per cent of Amazon's 2004 revenues coming from books, music and film, it was essential to Amazon's survival that it dominated the digital bookselling space in the same way that Apple did with music.

In the same year Bezos announced to colleagues that Amazon was developing its own electronic reading device. It was a radical departure from the company's core retail skills, but Bezos believed that to succeed, Amazon needed to control the whole customer experience – combining well-designed hardware with an easy-to-use digital bookstore.

The goal was to have 100,000 titles, including 90 per cent of *The New York Times* bestsellers, available for download at launch. Immense pressure was put on book publishers to digitise not just current titles, but large parts of their back catalogue. As Amazon's importance as a bookseller grew, so did their economic power over publishers. Removing a book from its 'recommended titles' list could cost a publisher up to 40 per cent of its sales.

When Bezos introduced the Kindle in November 2007, he announced that Amazon would be selling e-books for just $9.99 (£6.40) each – undercutting publishers' own hardbacks and taking a massive chunk out of their profits. Amazon quickly took a 90 per cent share of the digital reading market, and five major US publishers – Penguin, Hachette, Macmillan, HarperCollins, and Simon and Schuster – tried to break Amazon's dominance by striking a deal to sell e-books through iTunes at mutually agreed prices, with Apple taking 30 per cent commission on sales.

In turn, Amazon reported the publishers to the US Department of Justice for price fixing, and in April 2012 the courts found in Amazon's favour. Nevertheless, the argument over e-book pricing continues, and publishers are searching for ways to break Amazon's digital dominance of the market, and reach out directly to book and e-book buyers.

US Attorney Generals announce an anti-trust lawsuit against Apple in April 2012 for setting e-book prices too high.

Tom Hobbs and Symon Whitehorn
Kindle designers

British designers Hobbs and Whitehorn worked at design firm Pentagram, and spent several years developing the first Kindle with direct input from Jeff Bezos himself. As part of their research, they studied how people turn pages and hold books in their hands. At Bezos' insistence, a keyboard was added to the first Kindle's design.

> " The Internet is disrupting every media industry… People can complain about that, but complaining is not a strategy. "
>
> **Jeff Bezos**

what does the future hold for Amazon?

Amazon is one of the world's most successful e-retailers, with $67.86bn (£43.1bn) in revenues in 2013, compared to just $18.3bn (£11.6bn) from its nearest competitor, Apple. So where does Amazon go from here? Jeff Bezos has already taken the brand from books to mobile phones, so here are our predictions for Amazon's expansion in the next ten years:

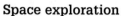

For around £200 per year, AmazonFresh subscribers have access to all Amazon Prime services, and same-day delivery on groceries.

Space exploration

It sounds fantastical, but Jeff Bezos' fascination with space goes back to high school. What we know for sure is that Bezos has formed a new company, Blue Origin, devoted to space exploration and is 'working to lower the cost of space flight to build a future where we humans can explore the solar system first hand and in person'. Amazon in space? We wouldn't bet against it!

Delivery by drone

Bezos introduced Amazon Prime Air on a US news channel, and the YouTube video has now been watched 15 million times! This 30-minute aerial delivery service by miniature flying robots won't be legal in the US for a number of years, but as soon as it is... watch out for Amazon drones overhead. https://www.youtube.com/watch?v=98BIu9dpwHU

Amazon supermarket

Amazon's grocery service, AmazonFresh, has recently expanded to California, after a five-year trial in Seattle, and is the company's attempt to grab a slice of the $1tn (£600bn) US food market. Revenues are slowly rising – a 23 per cent increase for the second three months of 2014 – so don't be surprised to see AmazonFresh deliveries reaching Britain and the rest of Europe in the next few years.

An experimental Amazon drone: is this the way we will see purchases delivered in the future?

> "This is Day 1 for the Internet. The alarm clock hasn't even gone off, and the world is asleep to what the rest of Day 1 will bring."
>
> Jeff Bezos, the *Observer*, 2014

Amazon's facts

237,000,000 The number of Amazon customer accounts worldwide

$189 (£120) Estimated spend of each Amazon customer over a lifetime, compared to $39 (£25) on eBay

162,000,000 Unique monthly visitors to Amazon sites

10,000 The number of Olympic swimming pools that could fit inside Amazon warehouses worldwide

73.7 per cent Kindle's share of the e-reader market

market a new Amazon service

When a company launches a great new product or service, it needs to create a marketing strategy to sell it to prospective customers. Imagine you're launching a subscription-based selection of Amazon television channels to challenge Sky. Here are the 10 important points you need to cover when writing your marketing plan:

Step 1: Put your plan in a nutshell
Briefly outline what you will include in your full plan. This will be useful to give you, and other readers, a quick overview.

Step 2: Who are your target customers?
Describe the customers you're targeting – their age, gender, interests, and what they want from a new TV channel or channels. Being able to clearly identify your target customers will help you pinpoint your advertising (leading to a higher 'conversion rate') and also 'speak the language' of prospective customers. For example, a TV channel featuring romantic comedy films would be advertised differently from a channel featuring Premiership football.

Step 3: What's your USP?
A strong USP helps you stand out from the competition. Amazon's USP is 'the everything store', but what would be the USP of its TV channels?

Step 4: Set your pricing and positioning strategy
Your pricing and positioning strategy go hand in hand. For example, if you want your company to be seen as a premium brand, then too low a price might make customers think that your product isn't top quality. What are your competitors charging, and what do they offer for the price? In this section of your plan, outline the position you want in the market, and how your pricing will support that position.

Step 5: What are you offering?

What special deals are you prepared to offer to attract customers to your service? Deals may include free monthly trials, money-back guarantees, or discount offers. Offering deals usually helps your customer base grow more rapidly.

Step 6: What's your promotions strategy?

This is one of the most important parts of your marketing plan, and explains how you will reach new customers. Methods include TV advertising, online advertising, press releases and so on – consider all the alternatives and decide which ones will help you reach your target customers.

Step 7: What's your conversion strategy?

How do you turn prospective customers into paying customers? If you're using phone marketing, your 'sales script' that the sales staff use to persuade customers to subscribe is vitally important. If you're targeting prospective customers by post, testimonials – statements from existing clients who have tried and enjoyed the service – can be useful. Think about what would work best for you.

Step 8: Spreading the word

If all your customers referred one new customer today, your service would double! To encourage customer referrals, prepare a referral strategy: will you ask all your customers? How often? Will you offer a reward or discount?

Step 9: Keeping customers happy

Many companies spend their time and energy attracting new customers, instead of focussing on existing customers. If you're offering a subscription service like a TV channel, you need to retain existing customers, and ideally entice them to spend extra money on one-off events. A monthly newsletter or customer loyalty programme can increase revenues and profits by getting customers to purchase from you more frequently.

Step 10: How much money do you plan to make?

The final part of your marketing strategy is to make financial projections. Include the expenses you'll incur, and what the expected results will be in terms of new customers, sales and profits. Also include the expected results from your retention strategy.

Your financial projections won't be 100 per cent accurate, but you can use them to decide on which promotions expenses will be the most cost effective. Your projections will also set goals, for example customer retention rates, which you can strive to meet. Completing a marketing strategy is hard work, but worth it. Stick to the plan, and your sales and profits should soar. Good luck!

glossary

anecdote
A short, sometimes funny story about something that someone has done

bias
A preference for something

cloud computing
The use of technology, services or software on the Internet rather than software installed on your own computer

conversion rate
The number of sales of a product compared to the number of people who visit a website to look at that product

core skills
The most important or well-used skills of a person or company

diversify
To produce a range of different products or services, in order to succeed in more markets, or to protect against risk

dotcom
Relating to companies that do most of their business on the Internet

entice
To persuade someone to do something by offering them something pleasant

frugality
Only spending as much money as necessary

incur
To be made to lose money or pay a charge

innovative
Using new ideas or methods

instant gratification
Immediately satisfying a wish or need

leapfrogged
To have improved a position by going past others quickly

lucrative
Earning or producing a lot of money

maximise
To make something as big or important as possible

middleman
A person or company that buys goods from the company that has produced them, and makes a profit by selling them to a store or to a user

overview
A short description of something providing general information, but no details

patent
The legal right to be the only person or company to make or sell a product for a particular number of years

perks
Advantages, such as money or a company car, that you are given for doing your job

pinpoint
To discover or describe the exact facts about something

proclaiming
Announcing something publicly or officially

reappraised
To examine a situation or activity again in order to make it more modern or effective

referral
The act of recommending to someone a product or service that you have personally used

retailer
A company that sells goods to the public, either in stores or on the Internet

royalties
Payments made to a writer, musician, etc every time something they have created is used or bought by others

troubleshooter
A person whose job is to solve problems for a company

undercutting
Selling goods or providing a service for a lower price than someone else

virtual
Something that can be done or seen using computers or the Internet

further information

Books

The Everything Store
by Brad Stone (Corgi, 2013)

One Click: Jeff Bezos and the Rise of Amazon.com
(Portfolio Penguin, 2012)

Web

Jeff Bezos interview in technology magazine *Wired*

http://www.wired.com/2011/11/ff_bezos/all/

Videos

Jeff Bezos interviews on YouTube

https://www.youtube.com/watch?v=YlgkfOr_GLY

https://www.youtube.com/watch?v=pEZqCuEEMdU

First published in Great Britain in 2015 by Wayland

Copyright © Wayland, 2015

All rights reserved.
Dewey Number: 381.1'42-dc23
ISBN: 978 0 7502 9261 0
Ebook ISBN: 978 0 7502 9262 7
10 9 8 7 6 5 4 3 2 1
Printed in China

Wayland
An imprint of Hachette Children's Group
Part of Hodder & Stoughton
Carmelite House
50 Victoria Embankment
London EC4Y 0DZ
An Hachette UK Company
www.hachette.co.uk
www.hachettechildrens.co.uk

Editor: Elizabeth Brent
Designer: Grant Kempster

Picture Credits: Cover: Brendan Howard/Shutterstock.com (left), Frank Gaertner/Shutterstock.com (right); p4: Thinglass/Shutterstock.com; p5: PhotosJC/Shutterstock.com (top), John MacDougall/AFP/Getty Images (bottom); p6: Everett Collection/REX; p7: Tang Yan Song/Shutterstock.com; p8: Northfoto/Shutterstock.com; p9: 360b/Shutterstock.com (left), Janne Hamalainen/Shutterstock.com (right); p10: Natalie Fobes/CORBIS; p11: KPA/Zuma/REX; p12: Gil C/Shutterstock.com; p13: David Paul Morris/Bloomberg via Getty Images; p15: Gil C/Shutterstock.com (top), mandritoiu/Shutterstock.com (bottom); p16: Barry Blackburn/Shutterstock.com; p17: Sipa Press/REX; p18: PA; p19: Sipa Press/REX, Sean Gallup/Getty Images; p20: Kevin P. Casey/Bloomberg via Getty Images; p21: Asif Islam/Shutterstock.com; p22: Liang Zou/Shutterstock.com (top), James Looker/Future Publishing via Getty Images (bottom); p23: Krisztian Bocsi/Bloomberg via Getty Images; p24: Andrew Harrer/Bloomberg via Getty Images; p25: Brendan Hoffman/Getty Images; p26: Kevork Djansezian/Getty Images; p27: DPA/PA; p28: irin-k/Shutterstock.com

Disclaimer: Every effort has been made to trace the copyright holder but if you feel you have the rights to any images contained in this book then please contact the publisher.

Please note:
The website addresses (URLs) included in this book were valid at the time of going to press. However, because of the nature of the Internet, it is possible that some addresses may have changed, or sites may have changed or closed down since publication. While the author and publishers regret any inconvenience this may cause to the readers, no responsibility for any such changes can be accepted by either the author or the publishers.

The author would like to acknowledge this source: *Chart on p11 adapted from http://www.statista.com*

DISCOVER THE INCREDIBLE STORY OF THE BUSINESS BEHIND THESE WORLD-FAMOUS BRANDS

978 0 7502 9264 1

978 0 7502 9261 0

978 0 7502 9252 8

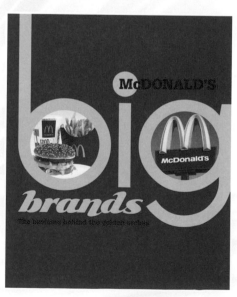

978 0 7502 9255 9